Saving Your Home through Loan Modification!

Saving Your Home through Loan Modification!

Edward Woods

To order additional copies of this book, contact:
Xlibris Corporation
1-888-795-4274
www.Xlibris.com
Orders@Xlibris.com
60003

Contents

While this book has been prepared with great care and research, it must be mentioned that there are no guarantees in finance. While the likelihood of success is very good by using this instructional book, the final outcome will depend on the situation that exists between you as an individual and your lender. It should also be mentioned that your lender will need to see that you have the ability to make the newly agreed-upon payments, so proof of your income will need to be provided. It should be stated that the laws of your state will determine what rules your lender must follow during the foreclosure process. It should not be inferred that the author in any way is suggesting that a borrower intentionally holds back mortgage payments in order to obtain a loan modification. Finally, it is not the intention of the author to suggest that a borrower who is in default should not seek out the advice of an attorney to assist them in making the proper decision.

PREFACE

IN THIS BOOK, you will begin to see the true nature of lending and what it means to you. Lenders make home loans for one reason. You guessed it! Lenders loan money in order to make money. This is a basic economic principle that has worked for banks and mortgage companies for decades.

For example, if you were to borrow $200,000 at an interest rate of 6 percent for a thirty-year term, your monthly payments would be $1,199.10. Of this amount, you would be paying interest of $1,000 per month. So just for the privilege of borrowing this money, you would pay $12,000 per year to your lender. In addition to this, you are usually paying about $25 per month to the lender in order to service the loan or to collect the payments and keep the books.

Now, does this mean that the lenders are the culprits here? Of course, they are not! We live in America, which is the very best country to live in for many reasons! One of the first things that we must appreciate is the ability to buy your own home in the first place!

In many countries across the globe, home ownership is just a dream that will never be realized. Even under the worst-case circumstances of an actual trust deed sale (we will cover this shortly), a customer will be disqualified from a new home mortgage for about three years. My goal is to give you a method that will avoid foreclosure in most cases and let you keep your home. Finally, while it is very probable that other options will be embraced by your lender that will allow you to keep your home, foreclosure is always an option for a lender.

In a market of prosperity, it is likely that a lender would follow through with a foreclosure if the borrower is seriously behind in payments. That is not the way it is now or the way that it will be for a long time! You see, the lenders are in the business of loaning money, not owning homes! There is a way to break through the standard collection mindset if you know how to do it.

It is our hope that you will read and understand the following instructions on how to accomplish your goal of keeping your home and, in most cases, actually lowering your mortgage payments. While the knowledge on how to accomplish this can be found in this book, the secret to using the information is to be found within you! So we wish you good fortune and peace of mind. May each new day supply you with new wisdom!

FOOD FOR THOUGHT

T HIS BOOK IS dedicated to those who need help and those who want to handle their own affairs to the best of their abilities. It can be said that no person can survive happily as an island. From time to time, we all need the advice or guidance of another. In truth, help is merely one human being reaching out to help another.

It is with this in mind that I want to thank my wife, Pamela, for her love and support. Many times, an author mumbles to himself or herself about the proposed content of the project that lies before them. It is often a welcome and necessary blessing to have your partner nearby to remind you that your cause is just! In keeping with this subject, you can count on the fact that the instructions and information included in this book have been disclosed by a competent professional with many years in the real estate and lending industry.

It is through this knowledge and experience that I created my company (EW Mortgage Solutions). By working in the loan modification industry, I have become very good at knowing what the lenders want. Let us also mention one more time that each situation is unique and that one should always keep all of your options open. While I am very confident that you can accomplish your goal on your own, it is never a bad idea to remember that other options, such as bankruptcy or a loan modification firm, do exist should you require them.

Since you have an opportunity to save your home by using this book, it is appropriate that you understand a little about the mindset of the lender.

It is also important to understand the true definition of the words *loan modification*. In this new world of massive debt, bank closings, and Wall Street failures, it is not in the lender's interest to provide more assistance than what the homeowner actually needs. What the lender will most likely do is provide the homeowner with enough assistance to make their mortgage payment! So having said this, the true meaning of a loan modification is as follows.

Your lender will assist you in making a payment that you can barely afford. This will be the lender's position because the last thing that they want to do is help the borrower to increase their disposable income, which would give the borrower more incentive to add new debt. I trust that you will be perfectly capable of using this information in the best possible way. Remember to always ask for the *loan modification department*, even when you know that you are still talking with the collection department.

In addition, be steadfast in asking for a long-term modification. In today's market, a good modification will last at least five years. Many lenders are currently asking for a short-term forbearance agreement before they will allow a long-term agreement. Since over 45 percent of past loan modifications have been ending in default, the lenders do want to make sure that a borrower can make the agreed-upon smaller payment first.

Since this is a common agreement, you shouldn't feel as though you are getting a less-than-satisfactory offer simply because you did not retain a loan modification company. Finally, just keep in mind that the purpose of a loan modification is to keep you from losing your home and not to allow you to save more money at the lender's expense.

Sincerely,
Edward Woods
EW Mortgage Solutions

MORTGAGE TERMS

*F*ORECLOSURE: AFTER A notice of default is recorded, the borrower has ninety days to cure the delinquent amount before the property is sold. The lender does not have to sell the property even though they have filed a notice of default. They usually will choose to work with a delinquent borrower where possible.

Short sale: In this case, the borrower is behind on their payments, and the lender may accept an offer from another buyer even though the amount of the offer is less than what the current owner owes the lender.

Deed in lieu of foreclosure: In this case, the borrower offers to give the property back to the lender, and the lender accepts the offer.

REO property: This type of transaction is a bank-owned property that has been taken back by the lender. In this instance, the offer from a new buyer is presented to the bank, and a decision is made as to whether or not they will accept the offer or counter the offer.

Workout program: On a workout program, the lender will give the borrower a chance to catch up on payments and, in some cases, even change the interest rate in order to accommodate the borrower.

Forbearance agreement: Here, the lender agrees to give a borrower up to eighteen months to catch up with past payments while keeping current payments active.

Military indulgence: If a person entered into a mortgage as a civilian and then later entered into the armed forces, they may be granted a military indulgence. This program comes with two offers. These are a lower interest rate and a long-term forbearance.

Loan modification: This is the best of all worlds for most borrowers since it changes the terms of the loan and puts any delinquencies at the end of the loan. In other words, the delinquent payments are capitalized. In most cases, the interest rate is reduced and placed on a fixed rate product.

NEW BAILOUT BILL TO THE RESCUE

I HATE TO be the one to break the news, but the new bailout program will not help everyone! After the final details emerge, they will disclose the truth (there really is no Santa Claus)! Hide the kids! Let's go through what we now know about the new program.

As far as the refinancing help is concerned, your home loan must be owned by Fannie Mae and/or Freddie Mac! If this is your situation, you must then qualify. This new program will allow the government to direct the loan process to the point where they will help with refinancing a new loan for you even if you are up to 105 percent upside down. Let's look at this example!

Your home is worth $215,250, and you owe $250,000; so far, you qualify to go to the next step! However, most people are far more upside-down than that. And if you exceed the 105 percent, you won't qualify! Next, your income must qualify to be in the proper range. Credit requirements will need to be disclosed.

Our next program designed to help homeowners will allow a bankruptcy judge to write down the mortgage balance in order to accomplish a payment plan that the customer can handle. It is possible that the judge may choose not to use this option if the plan can be successfully structured without it. If this option is used, the repayment process will likely last for years. In addition, the president's plan includes a mortgage modification option if certain conditions are met.

Very little discussion has occurred about the way to handle second or third mortgages. It has been stated that any government aid will place limits on how much devaluation they will try to cure. In other words, if you are too far down on your equity, you may be left out of the government program. Let us assume that you will qualify for this program.

Since any government involvement here will involve modifying your mortgage, doesn't it make sense that you should understand the process of how a loan modification works? So again, I commend you for taking the first step by purchasing this book, especially if you don't fit into one of the programs that will be coming. Now, let's look at some of the past government bailout attempts! One such plan was called HOPE for Homeowners.

This plan was designed to allow the government to buy your mortgage through a new FHA loan. The problem here is that hardly anyone was able to get this loan through because it required a lender to accept 90 percent of the current value as payment in full (if they were to accept this program). Is there any wonder why this program wasn't successful? Let's say that you owed the bank $300,000; and your new approval was based on the new current value of $200,000 times 90 percent, which equals $180,000.

This is a great deal, right? Yes, it is a great deal for the homeowner but not the bank! Since the only way that a lender can be forced to comply with this type of program is by compensating the bank for huge losses, it stands to reason that the new plan will not be a "golden parachute" for everyone either! In fact, it is now believed that a person would be better off by learning what the loan modification process is all about and planning on using this option to cure the problem.

HIRING AN AGENCY OR LAW FIRM

W HILE IT IS my position that you can accomplish a great deal on your own, I feel that I would be remiss in my duties to you if I did not explain some basic information regarding your other options. Most agencies that offer loan modifications retain an attorney or law firm. In some cases where applicable, it is customary for the attorney involved to examine the original loan documents to make sure that no errors exist in them. Should some error or technical glitch be found in these documents, it is possible that some relief may be realized that may afford some sort of strategy by which a homeowner who is experiencing trouble may find some legal way of avoiding or deferring the lender's demands.

Once again, should this option be attractive to you, it will not be free; and it will not involve a guaranty of success. It is not uncommon to pay $3,000 to $4,500 for this service, depending on how many loans you have on your home. Usually, if you have this kind of money, you will have paid your mortgage current in the first place! In some cases, it may be necessary or someone may be interested in consulting a bankruptcy attorney.

If this option is chosen, there are different approaches that the attorney may use in an attempt to help his client. Since practicing law is not my privilege or intent, I will leave it at that! There has also been a recent trend by agencies toward the avoidance of taking on new clients if a notice of default has been filed! Once again, this would be up to you if you were to choose to investigate these options.

It is safe to say that there are some differences between an agency that offers loan modifications and a law firm that offers bankruptcy services. Just keep in mind that these services do exist should you feel that they are needed. Keeping with the concept of freethinking and the right to explore your options, it can be stated that choosing this book is a wise move on your part. By becoming educated on what the solutions to a problem are, you will find that you are much more likely to make the right decision for you as an individual.

LOAN NEGOTIATIONS

W ELCOME TO THE secret process of loan negotiation! In every aspect of life, it is the method of doing a certain thing that makes it possible to accomplish the most difficult task. Remember the old story about pounding the square peg into the round hole? How about trying to start your car with the key to your spouse's car?

Our point here is very simple. In order to have success in dealing with the bank, you must have the right tools. Let's start by telling the lender who holds your mortgage a little about your situation. Let's cover the reason that you are in trouble as well as how you plan to be able to get back on your feet if you get the help from them that you need.

It is very important that you keep focused and calm during this process. You must remember that you are asking the lender to waive an interest rate that was agreed to when you signed your loan documents. It will serve you well to be both humble and reserved in your responses to sometimes-cranky representatives. If you maintain your calm attitude, it will reap you rewards.

Your goal here will be to not only ask the lender to place all back payments at the end of your loan (in other words, add to the loan balance) but also you are asking them to skip a payment and set up a new permanent loan agreement at a lower rate! If your loan is about to adjust, you are really in need of the new loan agreement or *loan modification*. Let's briefly talk about the difference between a loan modification and a loan forbearance.

When a lender grants a loan modification, the terms of the original loan are modified to reflect the new terms. In a loan forbearance, the lender allows the back payments to be collected in monthly payments, which are added to your normal regular payments. In other words, a loan forbearance has higher monthly payments because you are paying both your normal payment and your portion of the back payments.

So are you ready to start the process that will lead you to the solution you have been looking for? Let us move on to the part that will open up the doors and start the process!

PREPARING TO CONTACT THE LENDER

COMPLETE YOUR FINANCIAL statement. You will also want to gather your proof of income, such as W-2s or tax returns. Most lenders will want to see the last two months of your bank statements.

Prepare your proposal letter to the bank. You can use one of the sample letters that I have enclosed. Fill in the appropriate information that is specific to your situation. This gives the lender a reason why they should work with you. Be specific about what caused the problem, and most importantly, be sure to emphasize the reasons why things will improve once some help is provided.

Keep records of all correspondence. You will need to refer to your notes as you go through the process. You will need your loan number; address, of course; home phone number; and Social Security number each time you call in. Remember to be nice, and don't blow it by getting angry. It will be challenging because you will seldom get to speak with the same person until the file is actually assigned to someone.

Get any offers from the lender in writing. Verbal agreements won't get you very far because you will not be able to depend on them.

Do not be afraid. Do not allow the attitude of someone negative to deter you. At the same time, do not assume that a nice person will necessarily be the one to finally grant you an agreement. Stay focused, and do not get discouraged.

Know the process of foreclosure proceedings. I will cover this in the following pages. Knowing these things will help you understand what your options are and will also help keep the mystery out of your next move. Finally, it is necessary that you stay focused on your goal!

Remember that equity is very important! If you have enough of it, the lender may be less willing to work with you!

TAKING ACTION

B EFORE YOU REALLY begin to approach your lender for a workout solution to your mortgage problem, you need to be prepared. In the sample form section of this book, you will notice what I call a financial report. This is a simple form that tells the lender what your monthly debts are and what your payments are on each of these debts. Make sure that you complete this form in the most accurate way possible.

Your lender will use this form to determine a possible offer to you in the form of a restructuring of your loan. Once you have completed this form accurately, you will want to hold on to it since the lender may ask you several times to fill out their own version of this form. Make sure that you accurately explain why you are having trouble making the payments on time (see sample letter 1). When these two documents are ready, it is time to start the negotiation process!

Remember to be nice and to hold back any urges that you may have to tell someone where to go! There are several different options that are possible when dealing with the lender. First, you may be offered a loan solution that will ask you to send in money in different parts. For example, if you are one month behind, you may be asked to pay not only your next month's payment, which is due on the first of the month, but also a portion of the payment that was due the previous month.

This method is known as a payment arrangement plan. This is a common method and does offer the quickest way to come to a solution. If you find yourself in a position that will make it impossible for you to pay both your original payment and your deficiency balance from back payments, you are in need of a *loan workout program*. Those who have a loan that is going to adjust or has a high rate may find themselves in need of the actual modification of the existing loan, hence the term *loan modification*.

Under the loan modification program, the bank will actually change the terms and conditions of the loan in order to keep the customer from getting further behind. For example, the current rate is 6.8 percent on a three-year fixed rate loan. On the adjustment date on, say, May 1, the rate will go to 8.3 percent for the next six months. In an effort to keep the loan viable for the customer, the lender will usually choose to freeze the rate adjustment for a specific amount of time, but you must ask for it!

PRACTICING YOUR PRESENTATION

"THANK YOU FOR calling, Lending Guru, can I have your loan number? Who am I speaking with?"

"This is Mr. Lucky."

"Mr. Lucky, can I have your loan number?"

"Yes, it is 0000-000000."
"Can I have your address? Mr. Lucky, may I have the last four numbers of your Social Security number? Can you verify your home phone?"

"Yes, it is 000-000-0000."

"Thank you, Mr. Lucky, how may I help you?"

"Well, as you can see, I am having trouble right now with my monthly payment. I was hoping that you may be able to help me lower my interest rate. You see, I was hurt, and I couldn't work for about forty-five days. I am supposed to return to work at the end of the month, which is about two weeks from now."

"Mr. Lucky, let me transfer your call to the proper department." (ring, ring, and ring again!)

"This is Patrick, can you verify your loan number? Can you verify your current address and phone number? Thank you, and who am I addressing? How may I help you?" (as if they don't know what you want!)

"Yes, Patrick, I was injured, and I fell behind, and I was hoping that you may be able to lower my payment because my loan is due to adjust next month, and I know that I won't be able to afford the higher interest rate. Plus, I was hoping that I could work something out, like maybe allowing me to put my back payment charges on the loan balance."

"Mr. Lucky, I see here that you are still due for last month. Can you make a payment by phone?"

"No, like I said, I have been hurt, and I don't have enough money to make a payment right now. That is why I called."

"Mr. Lucky, you do realize that after the first of the month, you will be sixty days behind, and then I can't guarantee that your loan won't be forwarded to the foreclosure department. Can you make half of a payment by, say, Friday, and the other half by the twenty-ninth?

"No, Patrick, if I had the money, I would send it. That is why I am asking you for help!"

"Mr. Lucky, I am going to refer this to the loss mitigation department, and someone will be contacting you shortly. Is there anything else that I can do at this point?"

"No, I think that is it for now, I guess? Will this department be able to help me?"

"Mr. Lucky, as I said, if you go to the sixty days status, we may forward it to the foreclosure department, but loss mitigation can be more specific."

Welcome to the major leagues! Are you ready for hardball? Don't worry, you are ready! You are ready because you have already read the book on lending!

You know that this is a procedure, not a final sentence of doom! You can expect a call within a few days from the *loss mitigation department*. Of course, you have already been talking to them. This is now the girl that sits next to Patrick (it's her turn now)!

So she will begin the same way that Patrick and the customer service person started. Yes, you must give all of your info again! Not only this time, but every time! She will begin by asking you if you can send in a payment.

But you are not worried because your answer will be the same as you told Patrick, which will be, "Dear Ms. Lender, as I told Patrick, I won't be back to work until the first of the month. This is why I am asking for a lower interest rate and a loan modification. My loan is going to adjust, and I need the modification, not just the collection department."

"Mr. Lucky, I can only say that we don't want to be sixty days behind."

At this point you say, "You know, I have sent a request through certified mail that is asking for help. I mean, no offense to you, but I need someone that can help me to modify my loan, not just try to collect money like a collection agency." At this point, you say, "I am late for an appointment, so please see what you can do to help me. I will speak with you later. Thanks." then hang up.

Just a note! It may not be this bad! Just be prepared for a tough lender! It is very possible that the lender may be more anxious to make a deal than you!

STEP ONE

1. Gather your financial statement; your hardship letter; W-2 form for last year; a copy of any pay stubs or other income; your last two months of bank statements (all pages); and finally, any documentation that will support your request for help. For example, if you are injured or on disability you would supply a copy of this documentation.
2. Make photocopies of all documents and send the first batch by certified mail.
3. Call your lender and ask for the fax number of the loss mitigation department. Fax the same documents to this fax number.
4. Wait for a few days after you receive your certified proof of mailing and then call to ask for help. Remind the lender of your fax number and mailing address.

STEP TWO

1. Avoid giving way to pressure to send in money! Get a deal!
2. Prepare a copy of your tax returns for last year. Prepare any documentation that will show a return date to work or any supporting documentation to substantiate the status of any disability.
3. Continue taking notes of all conversations with each lender rep.
4. Ask for the loan modification department each time you speak with a lender representative.

STEP THREE

1. Send the second sample letter by both fax and certified mail.
2. Save all of your money! This will be part of your recovery!
3. Respond to any reasonable request for information by the lender.
4. Be polite on the phone, and don't panic!

MOVING FORWARD

T HIS FIRST LETTER that you will send to the lender is sample letter 1! When writing these letters, it is important that you address them to the loan modification department of your lender. It is better to address the letters to the mailing address on your mortgage statement even though it may not say loan modification department. After several conversations, the collector will have you fax information to them directly.

After about two weeks of conversation, it is time to send the second sample letter. Keep in mind that each and every time that you are about to hang up, you should request that someone from the loan modification department call you! Tell the representative on the phone in these early stages that you are aware that they are in the *collection* department and not the loan *modification* department; just be nice! Sometime between the first and second letters, you will be asked to forward your income information, such as your W-2 forms and a current pay stub.

These forms will be needed in order for the lender to make a decision on what type of program to offer you. By completing the financial statement in this book, you will have all of the income information at your disposal when it is requested. As was previously stated, it may be required by the lender that you use their forms; however, you will only have to copy the income information since you have already prepared your financial statement!

It is also very important to remind the representative each and every time that any agreement that is reached will need to state that any past due payments are to be *added to your loan balance*. You should also remind the lender that you are in need of a one-month pardon from making a mortgage payment. For example, if you are sixty days delinquent in April, then you will ask that your first payment be due on June 1! Don't be afraid of their response; you are negotiating!

At this stage, many lenders will have offered you a compromise of some sort. There will be a few lenders, however, that will still need some convincing. It may be possible that you will spend two months in negotiations! For these lenders, you will send sample letter 3.

If you will notice the gentle sway in this letter, it is basically saying you are sorry because you are sorry about everything! You are not happy that you have to ask these people for help. If it were up to you, the whole mortgage balance would be paid in full!

At this point, it is very important that you do stay on the nice side when speaking to the lender on the phone. In fact, you are so nice that you will even offer to fax a copy of all three letters to them! In some cases, after the third letter is sent by you to the lender, it is not uncommon for some time to go by before you hear something more. In many situations like this, some sort of plan is being discussed.

Each and every person will have a different set of circumstances at this stage. If you have saved your money since you stopped making payments, it is important that you hold on to this money. It could be that at least one payment may be necessary in order to actually get the agreement that you want. If you have just enough to make your first payment on your new agreement, then this absolutely must be hammered home to the lender!

If you have just enough money for your first payment, you should offer to prove this by providing copies of your bank statements. In some cases, you may be asked to speak to a lender that is recommended by the bank. If this happens, it is recommended that you comply with this request. It will actually convince the bank that no other options exist other than to provide you with some modification assistance.

It is very important that you remember the purpose of your efforts. It is not recommended or suggested that you negotiate in bad faith. In other words, making promises to the lender that you have no way of keeping is not the best thing or the right thing to do. It is understood how desperate things can get sometimes when panic sets in, and there is a fear that your family may lose their home.

Sometimes it is easy to fall into a trap that nudges someone to make a promise, thinking that the money will come somehow even when deep down it is known that this isn't the case. If unemployment is the problem, work extra hard to find something even if it is not the best job. After all, your goal is to keep your home, not put off the bank.

THE TWILIGHT ZONE

THIS IS THE time when you may seem unsure as to what happens next. You have sent the letters and talked with many representatives. You have been politely but persistently asking for help, and you are now waiting for a response. You have supplied documentation when the lender has asked for it, and now it is time to be rewarded for your efforts.

It is not uncommon for a drop-off in the collection calls at this point since it is now common knowledge that some type of compromise is pending. You have been hoarding whatever monies that you have to make sure that your new payment agreement will be met every month. Having said this, it is still possible that your lender may not be ready to compromise. If this is the case, you should be prepared to mail and fax the third letter one more time.

If this becomes necessary, it should be mentioned in this letter that there are many houses on or around your home that are for sale and vacant. In this case, you should drive around the block and make a list of at least five or six properties that are for sale and state in the letter that you do not want to become a statistic. Once again, you have an advantage because of the amount of foreclosure properties that are flooding the market.

You should, somewhere in your request for help from the lender, mention to them the advantage of helping you. After all, if they took the property, they would have to sell the property for what it is worth, not what you owe them! Your goal is to keep the house until the values come back, and then you would refinance the house and pay them off. This comment should be reserved for the third letter if needed.

Once again, it should be remembered that you are one of many victims of the housing crisis and a tough economy. It may seem like a small reason to feel good about yourself, but it is like filling out an application for employment during the Great Depression! Yes, you lost your job, but so did everyone else! Don't despair, and don't feel useless because you are human.

WRAPPING IT UP

A FTER YOUR EFFORTS have been spent, depending on your lender, you may feel as though you have not yet accomplished your goal. The truth is you have probably done much better than you think. One of the problems with lenders is that they are a very loose combination of employees who each has a job to do. Even though some employee of ABC Mortgage may still be coming at you from the same script as when you started, it doesn't mean that you have not made real progress in accomplishing your goal.

It takes a lot of time to gather all of the information together and get it to the proper decision maker. Remember that for most of your journey, you have been dealing with collectors even though they may have presented themselves as someone who will modify your loan. After a certain amount of time and effort (the amount of time depends on who your lender is), every lender will come to the end of the process. At this point, they will decide what type of offer to present to you.

So let's go over your completed steps. First, you gathered your documents that were needed, such as W-2s and pay stubs. Your next step was preparing your first letter to send to your lender and preparing your other monthly obligations and financial report, which lists all of your monthly expenses. Remember to emphasize the reason that you will be back on course with regular payments once the bank helps you by restructuring your loan.

It should also be mentioned that it may serve your cause better to designate a friend or family member that can act on your behalf to speak with the lender, should you feel that you are just not able to deal with the intensity of the negotiation process. If this is the case, you will need to address this in writing to the lender so that they can legally discuss your case with your designated person. Don't worry, this is not a chess contest against a master chess player! Just follow the basic instructions and contact the lender to work things out.

Our purpose in writing this book is to instruct you in the proper method of doing this without giving away the farm or making promises that are too difficult to deliver. When dealing with the bank, it is important to keep them focused on your needs and requests and not to let them stretch you like putty to fit their needs.

BOOK SUMMARY

I T IS MY hope that by reading the basic instructions in this book you have gained enough confidence to go forward in your goal to keep your home and reduce your monthly payments. Rest assured that many people have not purchased this book, and they have either paid someone a hefty sum to do the same thing that you can do yourself, or they have lost their home. Since you do have to live somewhere, why not let that be the home that you already have? In the highly unlikely event that you have done everything possible to work something out and it hasn't worked, you either have a lot of equity, which the lender wants, or you have not followed through with the plan.

If necessary and for some unknown reason that you were not successful, there is one last option that you can explore. This is where you would need the advice of a bankruptcy attorney or an agency that retains an attorney. I will say that you will be better off coming to an agreement with the lender on your own, especially if money is a problem for you. All of the forms that you have at the back of this book will help you to accomplish your goals.

Go forward with confidence and humility in realizing that we all need help from time to time. Unless you were born wealthy, there is a good chance that you have or will in the future struggle through some adversity. There is no shame in getting up off the floor when we are knocked down. In fact, once we have run through our time here on earth, we will not take a single cent with us. So be proud; be steadfast; and above all, *don't be afraid*!

Remember also that while we may have been trying for a permanent modification, some lenders will be somewhat reluctant to give you this. If this happens, don't be discouraged; just don't agree to anything that will restrict your ability to eventually refinance or sell the home. On the next two pages, I have included a sample of information about reverse mortgages. I did not include this information in the main body of our loan modification discussions because it will only apply to a select few.

Even so, I feel that it was important enough to mention. Just remember the product for your future reference.

REVERSE MORTGAGES

I F YOU ARE sixty-two or older, this program is one of the best and most beautiful things that could ever happen to you. To simplify the meaning of this product, I will provide a general overview of what a *reverse mortgage* means and how it relates to a home-saving *loan modification*. First, a reverse mortgage is a home loan that never requires a monthly payment. For example, let's say that a senior over the age of sixty-two, in some cases sixty, wants to pay off an existing mortgage of $100,000 with a monthly mortgage payment of $968. Under the reverse mortgage program, not only would that payment go away, but in many cases the lender would mail a monthly check to you without you ever having to repay any of it!

So let's say that you take out a loan when you are sixty-two years old, and you live to be one hundred years old. If you pass away at one hundred, let us also assume that you have received over $190,000 in monthly payments. And by not making a $968-per-month mortgage payment that you paid off thirty-eight years ago with the reverse mortgage, your total due for the bank for the reverse mortgage now comes to, let's say, $580,000. Let us say that your home is now worth only $350,000.

This is not a problem! That's correct; you leave no debt behind! Not for you, not for anyone! So who pays?

The answer is *your mortgage insurance pays*! Not your fire insurance, your mortgage insurance, which is an ever-present part of your FHA-backed reverse mortgage. In short, this is called an HECM loan. I would always advise getting this type of loan because it is backed by FHA, which makes it safe and dependable.

So let's discuss how this mortgage may help a customer who is in trouble and qualifies for the reverse mortgage. Let's say that a person doesn't quite have enough income to qualify for a loan modification but does have equity! For example, a senior has a house that is worth $240,000, and they owe $120,000. Under these conditions if given a chance, the lender would probably foreclose.

Fortunately for a senior in this position, the reverse mortgage would eliminate the need for any concern. Since there are no credit requirements to speak of, the new reverse mortgage would pay off the delinquent loan for good! Once your reverse mortgage is approved, you can forward a copy of the approval to your existing lender. This would not only stop the collection calls, but it may even cause your existing lender to treat you with respect again!

If the amount that is owed is larger, let's say that you owe $180,000; and your value is $255,000. You may still qualify if you are older. While a sixty-year-old customer may not qualify for this type of loan, a seventy-five-year-old just might make the cut. Finally, let's take a situation where a senior owes $170,000 and is forced to sell their home for $245,000 to escape foreclosure. In this case, by taking the profits from this sale and purchasing a cheaper home by using a new reverse mortgage, there would be no future payments! By doing this even though too much money was owed on the current home to qualify for the reverse, the new purchase price would be low enough for the down payment to qualify the buyer for a new *no-payment* reverse mortgage.

Let's use this scenario as an example. Mr. Yes will take his profit after the sale of, say, $60,000 after all expenses and use that money to buy a home for $120,000. In this market of declining values, this $120,000 home was selling for $235,000 just one year ago! When the purchase is complete using the reverse mortgage, there will be no payments! Once again, there is no need to worry about your credit rating when applying for this type of mortgage other than just making sure that there are no liens on the property.

I feel it necessary to mention this mortgage product in case you are one of the lucky few that did qualify for this loan. There are many unfounded rumors about senior citizens losing their home to shaky lenders who trick them, but if you choose a FHA HECM, you need not be concerned. Simply make sure that you keep your taxes paid and that you live in the home as your primary residence, and you will be fine. Remember that once you pass away, your family will not owe a cent under the FHA program!

In the following sample letter section, it should be remembered that each letter will serve as a basic format for your own situation.

OUT OF OPTIONS?

E VEN THOUGH IT is not in my nature to think negative, let's assume that you find yourself in a situation where you simply don't have any income! You have studied the Book, and have made all the necessary contacts, knowing that the job that has been promised to you is days away! You do have the Bankruptcy option, although as was previously mentioned, it is only a stop gap solution. I can assure you that in the case of Bankruptcy it pays to have all the details, so If you find yourself in this situation, you should consult an Attorney for details.

The other option is far more desirable to the bank, and will be better for you as well, in terms of doing the right thing. Let's say that you have no way to pay, and you do not want to stay in the house until the end, waiting for the Marshall to remove you. Why would anyone want this anyway? If this is the situation that you find yourself in, my advice is to contact the lender and offer them the option of giving them back the house in good condition.

You might say, why would I do that when I have no place to go? Our answer is simple! You need money to move, and if the bank will give it to you, in return for leaving the house in decent condition, why not take the money? This may sound crazy but it is very expensive for the Bank to foreclose.

Another additional reason for the Bank to consider your request for move out money, is the simple fact that many angry people intentionally damage the house! Many repairs are expensive, and it would make more sense to pay you something in return for your promise of cooperation.

Just for the record, this procedure is called (Cash For Keys). How much can a person expect?

When you consider the condition of some of the homes that are taken back by the bank, it makes sense for the bank to pay you at least $2500, and sometimes as much as $5000, to walk away and leave the house in marketable condition! Just keep this in mind if you are forced to have to start over!

SAMPLE LETTER 1

June 16, 2008

ABC Financial
Reference: Loan 211709-13-524589-3

Dear Representative:

I am writing this letter in order to explain why we are in a position of delinquency on our payments. Thor, my husband, has been on disability for some time now but is close to being able to return to work soon. We should be in a position to start making payments at that time, but we are hopeful that we can get some help with a lower interest rate and a transfer of any back loan payments into our loan balance. Every effort was made to get a new loan to refinance our home, but we were told that we either didn't have the equity or we couldn't prove income.

In total, we owe about $350,000; and we were told by the realtor that our house is worth less than that. I believe that the key is to help us with the back payments by placing them into the loan and extending a lower interest rate that will allow us to make timely payments until we qualify for new financing. Your help and understanding is very much appreciated.

Thor Moore
Dizzy Moore

SAMPLE LETTER 2

ABC Financial
Reference: Loan # 211709-13-524589-3

Dear Representative:

I am writing this letter in order to explain why we really do need your help. So far, we have been talking with people who are asking us to send in money that we don't have. Please believe me when I say that we do understand that we owe your company money. Our desire is to start a new payment with a lower rate.

It is our hope that any back payments can be placed on the loan balance. My husband, Thor, has been on disability for some time but is close to being able to go back to work. In the very near future, we should be able to start making payments on time if we can get some help with a lower rate and the placement of any back payments into the existing loan amount. Please know that being in this situation is very unpleasant for my husband and me, and we know that it is not what your company hoped for either.

Please forward this letter to someone who can help us with a loan modification.

Thor Moore
Dizzy Moore

SAMPLE LETTER 3

ABC Financial
Reference: Loan # 211709-13-524589-3

Dear Representative:

I wish that my husband and I were in a position to pay our mortgage to a current status. It has come to the point now where we are basically out of options. There is no other place for us to go for any help. It is true that we are truly in need of your help if we are to keep our home.

If you could modify our home loan and start a new payment schedule, we could begin making our monthly payments on time once again. It is our hope that you could place any delinquent amounts in our existing loan by raising the loan balance. If you could help us, we will recover and eventually pay off your existing loan with a refinance. Every time we go in town and around our neighborhood, there are foreclosures everywhere.

Finally, please know that we are truly sorry for being in this position and having to ask for your help. This is not the situation that we had hoped to find ourselves in. Your help would be a blessing.

Thor Moore
Dizzy Moore

FINAL THOUGHTS

Y OUR LIKELIHOOD FOR success increases dramatically if you follow these simple instructions. You are not alone! It so happens that you are one of several million people who are having trouble.

Don't count on the new bill in Congress! You still have to convince your lender to help you! You must also qualify for a new loan! Many people will not be qualified!

Every case is different! Much depends on who your lender is and how far you are behind!

Never negotiate in bad faith. In other words, don't agree to a loan modification if you are not receiving any income. How can you pay if you have no income! Most lenders will want some proof of your income anyway.

There are no guarantees in life! While most lenders will gladly work with you, there may be a small select group who will make it tougher for you.

Don't wait too long to act! It is probably not a good idea to wait until a few days before the sale date to contact the lender to work out payments unless you have a good sum of money that you are ready to pay them.

Some states have a judicial foreclosure process that gives you a full year to bring the loan current after the court foreclosure proceedings. Check on the laws of your state to see if this applies to you.

In California with few exceptions, you are not entitled to this feature! Your sale date is ninety days after the notice of default! This doesn't mean that the lender has to go to sale. This is where you come in to negotiate!

There are some exceptions to the judicial foreclosure process that relates to farms or other agricultural properties. Just remember that on a single family home, you are dealing with matters that directly relate to this book. There are other situations that relate to taking cash out and then going into immediate default that may cause a lender to pursue other remedies other than just foreclosing.

If you have doubts about what your situation may be, it would be advisable to consult an attorney. For the most part if you bought your home, even with two mortgages you are not likely to fear reprisal other than foreclosure as long as you lived there for two years. Just remember to check the laws of your state regarding any legal questions. It is really important that you pick up the phone and call your lender once you have familiarized yourself with this book.

Don't be afraid! Just go out and do it! If you have questions, stop and get the answers. In most cases, you can get this done by studying the material and going forward.

Hold your head up, and good fortune will find you! If you follow the instructions as given, you are very likely to enjoy success at a tiny fraction of the costs that you would incur by using an agency or law firm. After all, the price of this book is a great no-brainer alternative to your other options. Just remember that should you feel the need to consult an agency or law firm, you have the final say as to your course of action.

May you be truly blessed in all that you do! Think positively, and positive things will happen to you!

Financial Report

Home's current market value estimate $ _____

Existing mortgage balance   _____

Monthly gross income   _____
(husband and wife together)

Current mortgage interest rate   _____

Current mortgage payment   _____

Loan type (three-year, two-year, thirty-year)   _____

Number of months behind   _____

Total amount overdue   _____

Is there a second mortgage?   _____

Are there any liens on the house?   _____

How much did you pay for the house?   _____

Loan number   _____

Why are you behind on your payments?
(illness, loss of job, unexpected major losses, poor money management)

_____

_____

_____

_____

_____

Applicant's signature   _____

Coapplicant's signature _____

Other Monthly Obligations

Monthly food costs   _____

Monthly utilities   _____

Gasoline per month   _____

Insurance totals (nonmortgage)   _____

Auto payments (all vehicles)   _____

Phone bill   _____

Cell phone bill   _____

Cable bill   _____

Other   _____

Comments: _____

_____

_____

_____

_____

_____

_____

Keeping Notes

Date: /   /   /
Time: _____
Name: _____

_____
_____
_____
_____
_____
_____
_____
_____
_____
_____
_____
_____
_____
_____
_____
_____
_____
_____
_____

Keeping Notes

Date: /   /   /
Time: _____
Name: _____

Keeping Notes

Date: /   /   /
Time: _____
Name: _____

_____
_____
_____
_____
_____
_____
_____
_____
_____
_____
_____
_____
_____
_____
_____
_____
_____
_____
_____
_____
_____
_____

INDEX

I

interest rate, 7, 11–12, 17, 23–24
  lower, 12, 25

J

judicial foreclosure process, 49–50

L

Law Firm, 15–16, 50
lender, 11, 14–15, 17, 25–26, 30, 32,
   37–40, 49–50
  business of the, 8
  mindset of the, 9
  negotiating with the, 17, 21, 29
  problems with the, 34
lending, 7, 9
liens, 40
loan, 7, 12, 14–15, 17, 22, 24–25,
   39–40, 49
  refinancing a, 13
  restructuring a, 21, 34
loan agreement, 17
loan balance, 17, 24, 29
loan forbearance, 17–18
loan modification, 14–16, 22, 25, 27,
   29, 38, 49
  definition of, 10, 12

  difference between loan forbearance
   and, 17
  purpose of, 10
  relation between reverse mortgages
   and, 39
loan negotiations, 17

M

military indulgence, 12
money, 7, 15, 21, 24–25, 27, 30–31,
   37, 40, 49
money saving, 10, 28, 30
mortgage, 12, 14–15, 17, 39–40, 50
mortgage companies, 7
mortgage insurance, 39
mortgage payments, 8, 10, 39

P

payment agreement, 32
payment arrangement plan, 21
payments, 10, 14, 24–25, 30, 39–40, 49
  back, 17, 21
  late, 8, 11, 21, 29
pay stubs, 26, 29, 34
property, 11, 32, 40